Certificate III in Business

Assist with maintaining workplace safety

Core topic workbook

Linda Joel

A
FIVE SENSES
PUBLICATION

Five Senses Education Pty Ltd
2/195 Prospect Highway
Seven Hills 2147
New South Wales
Australia

Joel, Linda
Certificate III in Business
Assist with maintaining workplace safety
Core topic workbook

ISBN 978-1-76032-499-5

Contents

A glossary of key words for assessment

Using the glossary will help students to understand what is expected in responses in examinations and assessment tasks.

Account: Account for: state reasons for, report on. Give an account of: narrate a series of events or transactions

Analyse: Identify components and the relationship between them; draw out and relate implications

Apply: Use, utilise, employ in a particular situation

Appreciate;   Make a judgement about the value of

Assess: Make a judgement of value, quality, outcomes, results or size

Calculate: Ascertain/determine from given facts, figures or information

Clarify: Make clear or plain

Classify: Arrange or include in classes/categories

Compare: Show how things are similar or different

Construct: Make; build; put together items or arguments

Contrast: Show how things are different or opposite

Critically: Add a degree or level of accuracy depth, knowledge and understanding,
(analyse/   logic, questioning, reflection and quality to (analyse/evaluate)
evaluate)

Deduce: Draw conclusions

Define: State meaning and identify essential qualities

Demonstrate: Show by example

Describe: Provide characteristics and features

Discuss: Identify issues and provide points for and/or against

Distinguish: Recognise or note/indicate as being distinct or different from; to note differences between

Evaluate: Make a judgement based on criteria; determine the value of

© Five Senses Education Pty Ltd and Linda Joel

Examine:	Inquire into
Explain:	Relate cause and effect; make the relationships between things evident; provide why and/or how
Extract:	Choose relevant and/or appropriate details
Extrapolate:	Infer from what is known
Identify:	Recognise and name
Interpret:	Draw meaning from
Investigate:	Plan, inquire into and draw conclusions about
Justify:	Support an argument or conclusion
Outline:	Sketch in general terms; indicate the main features of
Predict:	Suggest what may happen based on available information
Propose:	Put forward (for example a point of view, idea, argument, suggestion) for consideration or action
Recall:	Present remembered ideas, facts or experiences
Recommend:	Provide reasons in favour
Recount:	Retell a series of events
Summarise:	Express, concisely, the relevant details
Synthesise:	Putting together various elements to make a whole

Chapter 1: Assist with incorporating WHS policies and procedures into work team processes

Short answers:

1. Identify the current legislation covering work health and safety in all workplaces in NSW.

   (2 marks)

   _____

   _____

2. Outline the duty of every PCBU with respect to WHS.   (2 marks)

   _____

   _____

   _____

3. Why are industry Codes of Practice developed?   (2 marks)

   _____

   _____

4. In a business services workplace, identify the risks that could impact on the health and safety of workers.

   (3 marks)

   _____

   _____

   _____

   _____

5. What are the differences between policies, procedures and programs?   (3 marks)

   _____

   _____

   _____

   _____

6. What WHS topics would generally be covered during induction training?   (5 marks)

_____

_____

_____

_____

_____

_____

_____

_____

_____

_____

_____

7. Why should WHS training be ongoing?   (2 marks)

_____

_____

_____

_____

8. Why is hazard identification and risk assessment important?   (3 marks)

_____

_____

_____

_____

9. When should hazard identification be carried out?   (3 marks)

_____

_____

_____

_____

_____

10. Explain the common categories of hazards. (6 marks)

_____

_____

_____

_____

_____

_____

11. Explain one method of communicating potential risks to workers. (2 marks)

_____

_____

Multiple Choice:

1. Who has the absolute duty to ensure the health and safety of visitors to a business?
    a. The PCBU
    b. All workers
    c. The cleaning crew
    d. The union representative

2. What documentation covers manual handling to help workers control the risk of injury?
    a. Legislation
    b. Union Publications
    c. Industry Code of Practice
    d. Australian Standards Publications

3. What is an identified risk in an office?
    a. Lack of ergonomic furniture
    b. Air conditioning set on 25 degrees
    c. Supplying headsets for answering phone calls
    d. Storing boxes in a separate room so workers have to walk 10 metres

4. Where can information be found relating to what workers have to do certain tasks and when they are to be completed?
    a. Procedure's manual
    b. Organisational policies
    c. Organisational programs
    d. Operating instructions manual

5. What is the primary goal of WHS policies, procedures and programs?
    a. To provide subject matter for ongoing training
    b. To protect workers from foreseen and unforeseen risks
    c. To give a worker a job to do rather than have them waste time
    d. To enable workers to understand what goes on in the business

6. At least how often should training be conducted on WHS issues?
    a. Daily
    b. Weekly
    c. Monthly
    d. Yearly

7. Why should ongoing WHS training be provided for workers?
    a. To introduce new workers to everyone
    b. To give workers a break from their usual job
    c. To inform workers of new and changing processes
    d. To enable workers from different departments to meet

8. What can reduce the likelihood of work-related accidents and ill health?
    a. Keeping plants out of the workplace
    b. Hazard identification and risk assessments
    c. Inspecting equipment and machinery every year
    d. Explaining why old machinery should be replaced

9. What is NOT a category of hazard?
    a. Biological
    b. Chemical
    c. Physical
    d. Sound waves

10. How should letters to individual workers about hazard identification be marked?
    a. Urgent
    b. Personal
    c. important
    d. For your eyes only

True or false?

11. The Work Health and Safety Act 2008 (NSW) is the current legislation covering work health and safety in all workplaces in NSW.

12. PCBU stands for person conducting a business or undertaking.

13. Industry Codes of Practice are generally accepted requirements to assist the smooth and safe operation of all businesses within that industry.

14. It is important that workers can perform their work safely and with risk.

15. Boxes stored in corridors can pose a risk to workers walking past.

16. At least half of the work health and safety issues covered in legislation must be included in organisational policies, procedures and programs.

17. Policies provide the steps to be followed in specific situations.

18. All workers generally undergo a period of induction training when they first start on the job.

19. Training should be ongoing to keep workers interested and motivated to reduce dangerous behaviour and eliminate hazardous situations.

20. Emergency evacuation procedures do not have to be covered in induction training.

21. The amount and frequency of training should reflect the level of risk involved.

22. Hazard eradication is part of the process used to evaluate if any particular situation may have the potential to cause harm.

23. Risk assessment can drastically reduce the likelihood of work-related accidents.

24. Equipment and machinery should be checked at the beginning or end of each shift.

25. Vapour from a photocopier is an example of a biological hazard.

26. The internet is a good way to communicate risks to workers.

27. Information on bulletin boards is often overlooked.

Write clues for the following completed crossword:

The crossword grid contains the following answers:

Down:
1. PSYCHOLOGICAL
2. EMERGENCIE
3. QUESTIONS
8. HAZARDS
11. INSPECTIONS
13. SURVEYS
14. FEEDBACK

Across:
4. RISK
5. BULLYING
6. CHEMICAL
7. INDUCTION
9. CONSULTATION
10. LEGISLATION
12. STANDARDS
15. PROCEDURES
16. ERGONOMICS
17. EMAILS

Across:

4. _____

_____

5. _____

_____

6. _____

_____

7. _____

_____

9. _____

_____

10. _____

_____

12. _____

_____

15. _____

_____

16. _____

_____

17. _____

_____

Down:

1. _____

_____

2. _____

_____

3. _____

_____

8. _____

_____

11. _____

_____

13. _____

_____

14. _____

_____

Answer the following crossword:

Across:

2. The steps to be followed in specific situations.

7. This is completed after a hazard is identified. (2 words)

10. A common type of hazard.

11. These are developed by industries.

13. This must be provided so workers can identify risks.

16. This should be done for all risks.

17. The person who should be informed about hazards.

18. Frequency of training that should occur.

19. A type of training.

20. This is important so nothing is left lying around.

Down:

1. These usually support legislation.

3. A method of communicating WHS information.

4. A physical hazard.

5. Follow up after training.

6. Covers lifting. (2 words)

8. These should be carried out regularly.

9. Completed after equipment has been tested.

12. This may be a hazard in an office.

14. A sit/stand desk is considered to be this.

15. This determines the amount and frequency of training. (3 words)

Extended response 1:

a) Differentiate between policies, procedures and programs. (3 marks)

_____

_____

_____

_____

_____

_____

b) Explain the primary goal of WHS policies, procedures and programs and how these are conveyed to workers. (4 marks)

_____

_____

_____

_____

_____

_____

_____

_____

_____

_____

_____

_____

_____

c) Explain why ongoing training is important in maintaining workplace safety and how is it best undertaken. (8 marks)

_____

_____

_____

_____

_____

_____

_____

_____

Assist with maintaining workplace safety

Extended response 2:

Explain how WHS legislation and Industry Codes of Practice leads to the development and implementation of workplace policies and procedures within the business services industry.

(15 marks)

Your answer will be assessed on how well you:
- demonstrate knowledge and understanding relevant to the question
- communicate ideas and information using relevant workplace examples and industry terminology
- present a logical and cohesive response

_____
_____
_____
_____
_____
_____
_____
_____
_____
_____
_____
_____
_____
_____
_____
_____
_____
_____
_____
_____
_____
_____

Assist with maintaining workplace safety

Chapter 2: Contribute to consultative arrangements for managing WHS

Short answers:

1. Why should every PCBU consult with workers about WHS?   (2 marks)

_____

_____

_____

2. How is a safe workplace more easily achieved?   (2 marks)

_____

_____

_____

3. When should workers be consulted about WHS?   (3 marks)

_____

_____

_____

_____

_____

_____

4. Distinguish between formal and informal consultation.   (2 marks)

_____

_____

_____

5. What is a benefit of conducting a survey about WHS?   (2 marks)

_____

_____

_____

6. What is the main benefit of conducting regular safety audits?   (2 marks)

_____

_____

_____

7. How can hazards be reported?   (2 marks)

_____

_____

_____

_____

8. Why should "near misses" be reported?   (2 marks)

_____

_____

9. Distinguish between an incident, an accident and an emergency.   (3 marks)

_____

_____

_____

_____

_____

_____

10. Why should workers be more involved in the day-to-day running of a business? (2 marks)

_____

_____

_____

11. What is open-door communication?   (2 marks)

_____

_____

_____

12. What should workers be encouraged to do with respect to managing WHS and why?

(3 marks)

_____

_____

_____

_____

_____

Multiple choice:

1. Who is most likely to recognise WHS problems in the workplace?
    a. The PCBU
    b. WHS consultants
    c. Experienced workers
    d. Managers when making inspections

2. When should workers be consulted about WHS implications?
    a. When coffee breaks should occur
    b. When the workplace layout is being rearranged
    c. Deciding who should be involved in workplace inspections
    d. Whether reporting of hazards should be done formally or informally

3. Who normally is elected to a WHS Committee?
    a. Owners, managers and union representatives
    b. Owners, managers and worker representatives
    c. Owners, union representatives and worker representatives
    d. Managers, union representatives and worker representatives

4. How often should a thorough WHS inspection be carried out in a workplace?
    a. Daily
    b. Weekly
    c. Monthly
    d. Yearly

5. How is a WHS audit usually completed?
    a. By using a checklist
    b. By talking to workers
    c. By walking around and looking
    d. By taking photos over time and comparing them

6. What is a formal method of reporting hazards?
   a. Speaking to the owner
   b. Talking to your supervisor
   c. Informing the WHS officer
   d. Filling in a hazard report form

7. What is an example of an incident?
   a. A worker slipping on a wet floor
   b. Burning toast setting off a fire alarm
   c. A worker's arm being caught in a machine
   d. A forklift knocking over boxes, injuring workers

8. What is an example of an advantage of encouraging worker participation in managing workplace health and safety?
   a. More ideas and creative solutions are discussed
   b. Workers can complete safety audits without supervision
   c. Serious problem will get out of hand before being identified
   d. A lot of money is saved by not involving outside consultants

True or false?

9. Worker input in WHS assists in reducing work-related injuries and disease.

10. A safe workplace is more easily achieved when one person is in charge of WHS.

11. Consultation results in more positive working relationships between management and workers.

12. Workers should be consulted when identifying hazards and assessing the risks to health and safety.

13. Formal consultation can occur when a manager has lunch with workers.

14. The PCBU must take on the role of WHS representative if workers are reluctant to take the role on.

15. Personal stories and case studies can be a powerful way of getting out the message about the importance of work health and safety.

16. Health and safety representatives attend training sessions on weekends.

17. A WHS inspection will look at signage, lighting and chemical storage.

18. Inspections of workplaces must comply with legislative requirements.

19. A dispute may occur when a health and safety issue is addressed.

20. Hazards may be reported during a staff meeting.

21. Reporting hazards enables the risk to be controlled as quickly as possible.

22. WHS policies must be regularly reviewed and updated.

23. An incident doesn't interrupt the normal running of a workplace.

24. Fire and Rescue is called when an accident occurs.

25. It is important to increase worker participation in managing workplace health and safety.

26. A workplace may become dangerous if workers are trained properly.

27. Encouraging worker participation in WHS means issues can be identified quickly.

28. By drawing on the knowledge and experience of all workers, more informed decisions can be made about how the work should be carried out safely.

29. Workers should be consulted when planning a new project.

30. Workers should be given the opportunity to provide feedback before changes are made.

Write clues for the following completed crossword:

```
                                        ¹A
                                         S
                        ²D E C I S ³I O N S
                                   N     S
                                   S     E
                                   P     S
                                   E     M
                                   C     E    ⁴W
                      ⁵P A R ⁶T I C I P A T I O N
                           R     T     N    R
                           A     I     S    K
                           I     O          R
                           N     N     ⁷I N F O R M A L
                           I                 S
                           N                 T
                      ⁸M O N I T O R I N G   ⁹U N R E S O L V E D
                           S                 R
                           E                 S
                           S              ¹⁰P
                           S        ¹¹S O L U T I O N S
           ¹²R I S K ¹³S            O        L
                     A              L        I
                     F        ¹⁴R   U        C
                  ¹⁵E F F E ¹⁶C T I V E N E S S   ¹⁷F   I
                     T        O     T        E    E   E
     ¹⁸E M E R G E N C Y      N     R             D   S
                     A        C  ¹⁹C O M M I T T E E
                     U        E     B             D
                     D        R     U             B
          ²⁰F A T A L I T Y   N     T             A
                     T        S     I             C
                                    O             K
                                    N
```

Across:

2. _____

_____

5. _____

_____

7. _____

_____

8. _____

_____

9. _____

_____

11. _____

_____

12. _____

_____

15. _____

_____

18. _____

_____

19. _____

_____

20. _____

_____

Down:

1. _____

_____

3. _____

_____

4. _____

_____

6. _____

_____

10. _____

_____

13. _____

_____

14. _____

_____

16. _____

_____

17. _____

_____

Answer the following crossword:

Across:

2. This is very important when setting up a new office.

7. Workers should be consulted when planning to buy this. (2 words)

8. The person who is ultimately responsible for healthy and safety in the workplace.

9. Workers should be encouraged to do this to ensure safety. (2 words)

10. Continued consultation with workers will build more of this.

11. An example of informal consultation. (3 words)

14. Regular inspections will reduce these.

15. Workers can identify problems as they go about this. (2 words)

19. A good methos to gather information about health and safety.

Down:

1. A forum where safety issues can be raised.

3. This should be taken when a hazard is identified. (2 words)

4. These should be reported, even if no one is injured. (2 words)

5. This should be done with workers rather than consulting on a case-by-case basis when issues arise. (2 words)

6. A method of reporting hazards.

9. These issues should be raised before they become a problem.

12. Health and safety representatives should attend these regularly to keep up-to-date. (2 words)

13. This should be inspected regularly in an office.

16. An important form of communication with managers. (2 words)

17. This should be done for minor problems before they turn into major problems.

18. Most accidents are generally this.

Extended response 1:

a) Explain the importance of consulting with team members when managing health and safety in the workplace. (3 marks)

_____

_____

_____

_____

_____

b) Explain how team members can contribute to the consultation and participation processes when managing health and safety in the workplace. (3 marks)

_____

_____

_____

_____

_____

_____

_____

_____

c) Explain why it is important to respond to WHS issues in a timely manner. (9 marks)

_____

_____

_____

_____

_____

_____

_____

_____

Extended response 2:

Explain how health and safety issues are dealt with according to organisational policies and procedures. (15 marks)

Your answer will be assessed on how well you:
- demonstrate knowledge and understanding relevant to the question
- communicate ideas and information using relevant workplace examples and industry terminology
- present a logical and cohesive response

_____

_____

_____

_____

_____

_____

_____

_____

_____

_____

_____

_____

_____

_____

_____

_____

_____

_____

_____

_____

_____

_____

_____

_____

Assist with maintaining workplace safety

Chapter 3: Contribute to organisational procedures for providing WHS training

Short answers:

1. Identify the work roles for which workers must complete specified training.　　(3 marks)

_____

_____

_____

_____

_____

_____

2. What determines the amount and frequency of training?　　(1 mark)

_____

3. What is generally included in initial health and safety training?　　(3 marks)

_____

_____

_____

_____

_____

_____

4. What is a Training Needs Analysis?　　(2 marks)

_____

_____

_____

5. Why is refresher training important?　　(2 marks)

_____

_____

_____

6. Differentiate between the three levels of training. (3 marks)

_____

_____

_____

_____

_____

_____

7. How has training changed over the last few years? (2 marks)

_____

_____

_____

_____

8. Why are some workers supervised on the job? (2 marks)

_____

_____

_____

Multiple choice:

1. When should hazard and risk identification be explained to workers?
    a) During induction training
    b) When someone points it out
    c) During a weekly staff meeting
    d) At an informal lunch gathering

2. What can a checklist be used for?
    a) Recording skills of workers
    b) Completing a Training Needs Analysis
    c) Making sure that every worker has correct safety gear
    d) To keep records of the WHS training every worker has completed

3. What is often covered in "refresher" training?
    a) Who the safety rep is
    b) Emergency procedures
    c) Who the stakeholders are
    d) How to use equipment correctly

4. What level of training would include information about compliance with legislation?
   a) Level 1
   b) Level 2
   c) Level 3
   d) Level 4

5. What level of training includes competency-based training to assess knowledge for the attainment of a certificate or licence?
   a) Level 1
   b) Level 2
   c) Level 3
   d) Level 4

6. What is the main benefit of completing training via connected real time delivery?
   a) You can Zoom in on people
   b) You only have to be dressed from the waist up
   c) It is less expensive than face-to-face meetings
   d) Provides for active participation between trainer and learner

7. What is a disadvantage of completing training via connected real time delivery?
   a) Verbal assessments must be done
   b) Everyone must keep up with the trainer
   c) Your kids can be seen mucking up behind you
   d) Some people take up too much time asking questions

8. When should on-the-spot awareness training be conducted?
   a) It is too hot to complete all the tasks scheduled
   b) A team member is not deemed as competent to do a task
   c) A supervisor notices that tools are not stored in correct order
   d) Team members start arguing about who is to complete what task

True or false?

9. Business policies and procedures stipulate workers must complete specified training and assessment before they can undertake certain work or roles.

10. Special training must be done for asbestos removal.

11. Induction training covers what happens when a worker is injured on the job.

12. Training is usually based on what the business owner can afford.

13. A Training Needs Analysis identify the gap between what skills are required and what skills the team members have.

14. Training on manual handling techniques usually takes place after someone is injured when picking up a heavy object.

15. HSR stands for High Safety Representative.

16. Level 3 training involves proficiency training.

17. A disadvantage of conducting training via Zoom or Skype is that pre-recorded videos cannot be shown.

18. Training for high-risk jobs cannot be done via Zoom but must be delivered face-to-face.

19. The originals of qualifications, certificates and licenses must be sighted and copies kept.

20. Supervision of workers only involves a supervisor standing and watching them work.

Write clues for the following completed crossword:

1 STAKEHOLDER
2 VERBAL ASSESSMENT
3 HAZARD
4 JOURNALS
5 ZOOM
6 FIRST AID
6 FORKLIFT
7 INDUCTION
8 COMPETENCIES
9 WORKSYSTEMS
10 SAFETY
11 FIRSTAIDSTATION
12 INCIDENTS
13 VIDEOCONFERENCING
14 SUPERVISORS
15 RISK
16 RECORDS
17 TEAMMEMBERS
18 TRAININGPLAN
19 SURVEYS

Across:

5. ____

____

6. ____

____

7. ____

____

9. ____

____

10. _____

_____

13. _____

_____

17. _____

_____

18. _____

_____

19. _____

_____

Down:

1. _____

_____

2. _____

_____

3. _____

_____

4. _____

_____

6. _____

_____

8. _____

_____

11. _____

_____

12. _____

_____

14. _____

_____

15. _____

_____

16. _____

_____

Answer the following crossword:

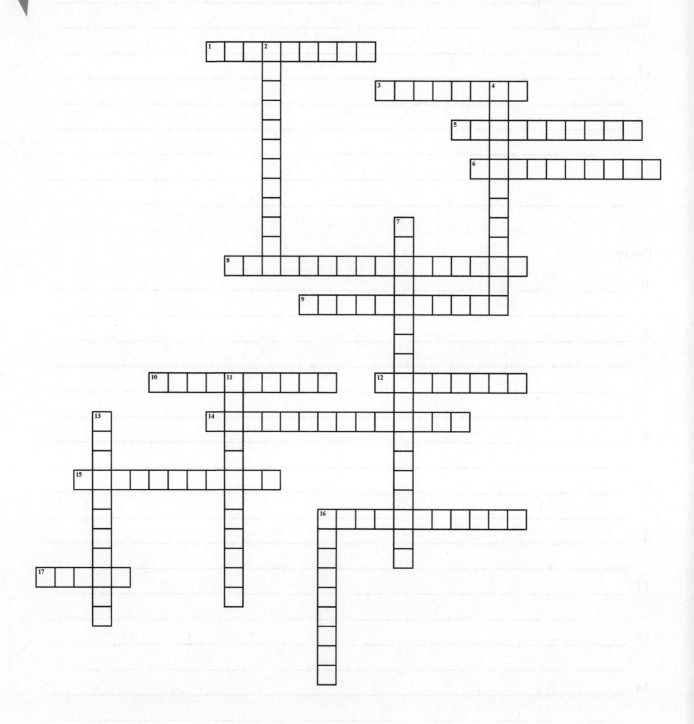

Across:

1. Training is mandatory to gain this certificate to work in the construction industry. (2 words)

3. Special training is required for these types of jobs. (2 words)

5. Workers who must complete refresher training relating to systems of work. (2 words)

6. This can suffer if incidents and accidents occur in the workplace. (2 words)

8. Health and safety _____ must be covered in induction training.

9. Training for these is very important.

10. Method of delivery of training.

12. A source of information used as part of training.

14. Refresher courses on this must be completed regularly to prevent injuries occurring. (2 words)

15. This stipulates workers must complete specialised training and assessment before they can undertake certain types of work.

16. This is usually obtained after Level 3 training is completed.

17. Reason why most training has moved to video conferencing.

Down:

2. Informal group discussions that focus on a particular safety issue. (3 words)

4. Health and Safety Representatives are an example of these.

7. Records must be kept to show that this has happened. (3 words)

11. This is formulated to cover gaps identified in a Training Needs Analysis. (2 words)

13. This must be provided for any worker not deemed fully competent at his/her job.

16. This is often completed during a Training Needs Analysis. (2 words)

Extended response:

a) Explain why it is important that workers complete WHS training. (3 marks)

_____

_____

_____

_____

_____

_____

b) Explain how team members can be supported until they have reached competence in their job. (3 marks)

_____

_____

_____

_____

_____

_____

_____

_____

_____

c) Explain the levels of training available and how these have changed in recent times, including any advantages and disadvantages. (9 marks)

_____

_____

_____

_____

_____

_____

_____

_____

© Five Senses Education Pty Ltd and Linda Joel

Assist with maintaining workplace safety

Assist with maintaining workplace safety

Chapter 4: Participate in identifying hazards, and assessing and controlling risks for the work area

Short answers:

1. What is a hazard? (1 mark)

_____

2. What is hazard identification? (2 marks)

_____

_____

_____

3. Where are hazards likely to be found? (2 marks)

_____

_____

_____

4. How can human factors be a hazard in an office? (3 marks)

_____

_____

_____

5. What other than hazards should be reported? (2 marks)

_____

6. What is a risk assessment? (2 marks)

_____

_____

7. What is risk control? (2 marks)

_____

_____

8. What is the best method for controlling risks? (2 marks)

_____

_____

9. How can risks be minimised? (3 marks)

_____

_____

_____

10. What safe work practices can be introduced to control risks? (2 marks)

_____

_____

11. When should hazard assessment and control methods be reviewed? (2 marks)

_____

_____

12. Other than using control measures, how can further inadequacies be identified? (3 marks)

_____

_____

_____

13. To whom should inadequacies be reported? (2 marks)

_____

_____

14. What can accident and incident reports identify? (2 marks)

_____

_____

15. What constitutes an incident? (2 marks)

_____

_____

16. When should an incident be notified to SafeWork NSW? (2 marks)

_____

_____

Multiple choice:

1. How can business equipment be a potential workplace hazard?
   a. Stacked boxes could fall on someone
   b. Noisy machinery can damage hearing
   c. Frayed cords could result in electrical shocks
   d. Unrealistic time frames can lead to increased stress

2. Whose responsibility is it to identify health and safety issues?
   a. Everyone
   b. The PCBU
   c. Team leaders
   d. WHS committee

3. What happens after a safety hazard has been identified?
   a. It is investigated
   b. It is reported and recorded
   c. A risk assessment is completed
   d. It is eliminated so no harm can be caused

4. Why is a risk assessment completed?
   a. To determine what harm could occur
   b. To determine what action should be taken
   c. To determine whether it really is a problem
   d. To determine whether it is a risk or a hazard

5. How can a risk be minimised?
   a. By eliminating it
   b. By using more PPE
   c. By modifying work practices
   d. By employing more specialists

6. What is another example of how risks can be controlled?
   a. Maintaining good records
   b. Increasing hazard identification
   c. Supplying legislative regulations to workers
   d. Carrying out regular emergency drills for all workers

7. Who should be responsible for ensuing that all new workers in a large business receive appropriate induction training?
    a. The CEO
    b. The PCBU
    c. The admin department
    d. The WHS representative

8. How can the effectiveness of control measures be evaluated?
    a. By consultation with workers
    b. By following safety information
    c. By meeting legislative requirements
    d. By better communication of safety standards

9. When should risk assessment be undertaken?
    a. Once a year on the same date
    b. When the business has a new owner
    c. When the layout of the premises is changed
    d. When internal and external audits are conducted

10. What is NOT an incident?
    a. Near misses
    b. Security issues
    c. Injured workers
    d. Property damage

11. What is recorded on an incident report form?
    a. The ages of those injured
    b. The legislation that covers the incident
    c. The person responsible for the incident
    d. The name of the person reporting the incident

12. What kind of control to minimise risk is a mechanical device that handles heavy objects?
    a. Administrative
    b. Engineering
    c. Isolation
    d. Substitution

13. For what does PPE stand?
    a. Personal Protected Equipment
    b. Personal Protective Equipment
    c. Personally Protected Environment
    d. Personally Protective Environment

True or false?

14. Hazards are anything that can cause harm to a person.

15. Under the *Work Health and Safety Act 2011* (WHS Act) every worker has the primary duty to manage risks to health and safety.

16. Hazard control is the process of examining the workplace to identify all potentially hazardous things or situations that may cause harm to workers.

17. Hazards are only found in the physical work environment.

18. Fumes from photocopiers can result in workers experiencing headaches.

19. Back strain can be caused by lifting items correctly.

20. It is important to immediately report anything that looks hazardous.

21. Workplace policies and procedures must reflect regulatory requirements when reporting and recording work health and safety issues.

22. All hazards reported should be recorded in a special book provided to the business by WorkSafe NSW.

23. A risk assessment should include an evaluation of the costs in rectifying the risk.

24. The first step in the hierarchy for risk control is to minimise the risk.

25. An example of substitution is making the load lighter by using smaller boxes.

26. Job rotation is an example of modification.

27. Evaluation ensures that all potential and existing hazards are identified.

28. Feedback from workers is important when implementing change.

29. There is no need to record follow up recommendations on incident or accident report forms.

30. WorkSafe NSW can be contacted from 7am to 7pm on work days.

Write clues for the following completed crossword:

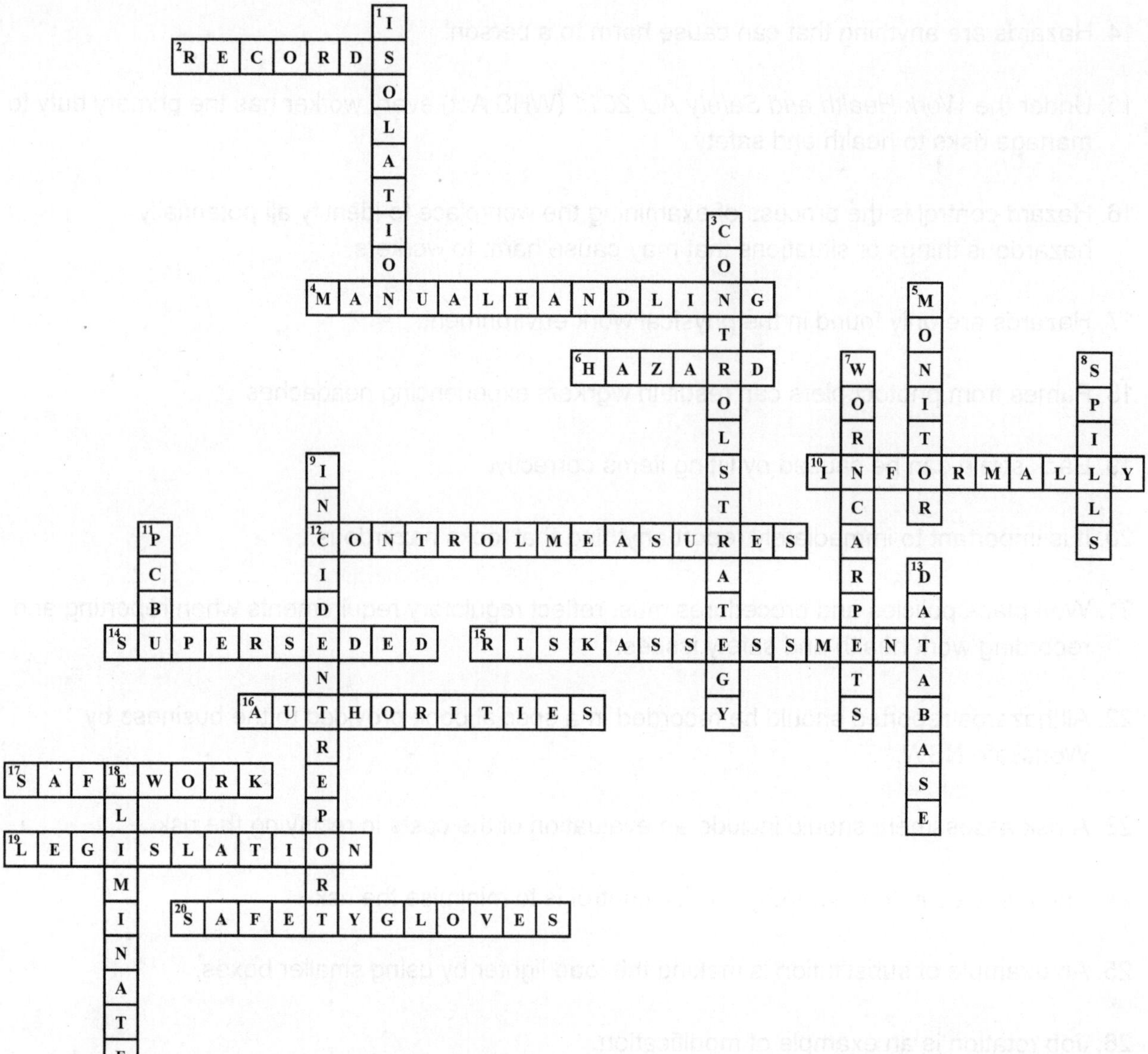
1 ISOLATION
2 RECORDS
3 CONTROLSTRATEGY
4 MANUALHANDLING
5 MONITOR
6 HAZARD
7 WORNCARPETS
8 SPILLS
9 INCIDENTREPORT
10 INFORMALLY
11 PCBU
12 CONTROLMEASURES
13 DATABASE
14 SUPERSEDED
15 RISKASSESSMENT
16 AUTHORITIES
17 SAFEWORK
18 ELIMINATE
19 LEGISLATION
20 SAFETYGLOVES

Across:

2. ______________________________

____

4. ______________________________

____

6. ______________________________

____

10. ______________________________

____

12. _____

_____

14. _____

_____

15. _____

_____

16. _____

_____

17. _____

_____

19. _____

_____

20. _____

_____

Down:

1. _____

_____

3. _____

_____

5. _____

_____

7. _____

_____

8. _____

_____

9. _____

_____

11. _____

_____

13. _____

_____

18. _____

_____

Crossword:

Across:

3. These incidents include a serious injury or illness.

6. This may happen if there are too many power cords on the one power point. (2 words)

8. Used to identify safety problems in the workplace.

11. Amount that can be charged for not notifying authorities of a serious incident. (2 words)

13. Using something with a lower risk.

15. Two things that must reflect regulatory requirements regarding safety issues. (2 words)

17. The person a worker reports a safety issue to.

18. Control measures should be reviewed when these are introduced. (3 words)

20. The person who comes when an incident is reported to the authorities.

Down:

1. Risk control should prevent this from occurring. (3 words)

2. This should be notified to authorities immediately.

4. Period of time records of notifiable incidents have to be kept. (2 words)

5. This will eliminate or control a risk. (2 words)

7. Details of these must be recorded on an incident report form. (2 words)

9. This can be a major source of headaches.

10. Risk control helps to do this. (2 words)

12. Introducing safeguards is an example of this. (2 words)

14. Sometimes these are unrealistic and can increase stress levels.

16. These people must be protected from harm in a workplace.

19. Type of process regarding risk assessment and control.

Extended response 1:

a) Describe the potential workplace hazards that could be found in a business services workplace. (3 marks)

_____

_____

_____

_____

b) Outline the process of risk assessment. (3 marks)

_____

_____

_____

_____

_____

_____

_____

_____

c) Outline how risks can be controlled once they have been identified. (9 marks)

_____

_____

_____

_____

_____

_____

_____

_____

_____

_____

Extended response 2:

Explain why hazard identification, risk assessment and control is an ongoing process and why it is important to keep records according to WHS legislative requirements.   (15 marks)

Your answer will be assessed on how well you:
- demonstrate knowledge and understanding relevant to the question
- communicate ideas and information using relevant workplace examples and industry terminology
- present a logical and cohesive response

_____

_____

_____

_____

_____

_____

_____

_____

_____

_____

_____

_____

_____

_____

_____

_____

_____

_____

_____

_____

_____

_____

_____

Chapter 5: Assessment tasks to provide evidence of ability and demonstration of knowledge of topic

Each student must provide evidence of the ability to:

- **assist with implementing and monitoring at least three different organisational work health and safety (WHS) policies or procedures into a work team's processes**

Each student must also be able to:

- **assist with implementing and monitoring consultation about each policy or procedure according to legislative and organisational requirements**
- **identify opportunities to encourage work team to contribute to implementing improvements to each policy or procedure based on feedback received through consultation**
- **complete WHS documentation**

Instructions:

Students are to work in groups of three or four people. Answer should be submitted on your own paper for marking. Only one copy for the group needs to be submitted, but make sure that every student in the group has a copy. Submitted answers will be marked as competent or not yet competent. Any task that is deemed not yet competent must be reviewed, updated and resubmitted until it has been deemed competent.

Preparation for task:

Go to the following websites and read the current policies for schools for:

- Excursions: https://education.nsw.gov.au/policy-library/policies/pd-2004-0010
- Swimming and water safety: https://app.education.nsw.gov.au/sport/page/1116
- Sport and physical activity: https://education.nsw.gov.au/policy-library/policies/pd-2002-0012

Task 1:

1. Write three policies that could be implemented into your school using the following headings:

   a) Policy statement
   b) Audience and applicability
   c) Context
   d) Responsibilities
   e) Monitoring and review

   Suggested topics: use of mobile phones; emergencies and evacuations; detentions; school reports; bullying; anti-discrimination; behaviour; homework; security; accidents at school; attendance; uniforms; handling mail.

2. In an addendum:

   a. Identify any legislation that must be taken into consideration before writing your policies.

   b. Identify who you would consult before writing each policy and after they have been written. Politely ask each person identified for their opinions on each of your chosen policies. Document the consultation process and identify suggested improvements.

   c. Outline how these policies would be implemented.

   d. Devise forms that would be required for documentation of your policies.

Each student must also demonstrate knowledge of:

- **characteristics and composition of the work team**
- **procedures related to the following:**
    - **identifying hazards**
    - **assessing and controlling risks to health and safety, including the hierarchy of control measures**
- **organisational WHS policies and procedures, including those relating to:**
    - **risk management**
    - **fire**
    - **emergencies**
    - **evacuation**
    - **incident investigation**
    - **reporting**
- **relevant legislation, regulations and codes of practice from all levels of government that impact on business operations, including those relating to:**
    - **WHS and environmental issues**
    - **equal opportunity**
    - **industrial relations**
    - **anti-discrimination**
- **WHS aspects of other organisational systems and procedures**

Instructions:

Each student is to complete their own answers for this section. Submitted answers will be marked as competent or not yet competent. Any task that is deemed not yet competent must be reviewed, updated and resubmitted until it has been deemed competent.

Task 2:

1. Teams:
   a) Define "team composition".
   b) Differentiate between homogenous and heterogeneous teams.
   c) How can age; gender; ethnic background; personality; and knowledge, skills and ability of team members affect the performance of a team?

2. Hazards: Choose one area of the school, inspect it and complete a hazard identification and risk assessment of the area. Document the process, including the hierarchy of control measures used.

3. WHS policies and procedures:
   a) Obtain a copy of the school's WHS policies and procedures on the topics in the list in Task 1.
   b) Review each policy and procedure and write a report on any inadequacies found.
   c) Identify the stakeholders who should be informed of your findings. Give a copy of your report to each stakeholder.
   d) If there is no policies and procedures on any topic, write a report stating why there should be policies and procedures written for each topic, outlining the key points that should be included for each topic. Give a copy of this report to the relevant stakeholders.

4. Legislation, regulations and codes of practice:
   a) Identify relevant legislation, regulations and codes of practice from all levels of government that impact on the operation of your school, relating to:
      • WHS and environmental issues
      • equal opportunity
      • industrial relations
      • anti-discrimination
   b) Write a brief summary of how each piece of legislation, regulation or code of practice affects the operation of your school.

5. Organisational systems and procedures:
   a) Identify the WHS aspects of ONE organisational system and its procedures operating in your school.

Chapter 6: Suggested answers

Note: no suggested answers are given for the completed crosswords as answers will vary for each student.

Chapter 1:

1. The Work Health and Safety Act 2011 (NSW) and the Work Health and Safety Regulation 2017 (NSW) are the current legislation covering work health and safety in all workplaces in NSW.

Marks	Criteria
2	• Identifies two current pieces of legislation covering WHS
1	• Identifies one current piece of legislation covering WHS

2. PCBU has an absolute duty to take all reasonably practicable steps to ensure the health and safety of workers, visitors, volunteers and any other persons impacted by the business, by the elimination or minimisation of any risk of injury to any person present in the workplace at any time for any reason.

Marks	Criteria
2	• Detailed outline of the duty of every PCBU to WHS
1	• Mentions at least one point of the duty of every PCBU to WHS

3. Industry Codes of Conduct are developed to govern the way that industry operates, to assist the smooth and safe operation of all businesses within that industry.

Marks	Criteria
2	• Detailed explanation of why Codes of Conduct are developed
1	• Mentions at least one point about why Codes of Conduct are developed

4. The risks that could impact on the health and safety of workers include:
   - Lighting: glare and inappropriate lighting
   - Ventilation: poor air flow and air conditioning
   - Handling equipment: manual handling problems
   - Electrical equipment: testing and tagging practices
   - Telephones: use of headsets verses telephone handsets
   - Furniture: lack of ergonomic furniture, including sit/stand desks
   - Computers and other electronic devices: suitability to task at hand
   - Storage systems: lack of storage, boxes and crates being stored in hallways

Marks	Criteria
3	• Identifies 7-8 risks
2	• Identifies 2-6 risks
1	• Mentions at least one risk

5. The policy sets out the ideas used as the basis for making decisions, the procedures provide the steps to be followed in specific situations, while the programs state more specifically who will do what and when.

Marks	Criteria
3	• Explains the difference between policies, procedures and programs
2	• Explains the difference between two of the above
1	• Explains what one of the above is

6. WHS topics generally covered in induction training could include:
   - An overview of WHS legislation, including the duties of all parties; who the WHS representative is and the WHS committee; key regulations and codes of practice
   - Workplace policies and procedures regarding topics like bullying and harassment; reporting hazards, incidents and injuries; equal opportunity; safe handling of hazardous substances
   - Major potential hazards in the workplace: potential effects, how to identify them and how they are controlled
   - First aid arrangements and identification of the first aid officer
   - Emergency evacuation procedures
   - Training specific to their job

Marks	Criteria
5	• Explains at least five topics
4	• Explains at least four topics
3	• Explains at least three topics
2	• Explains at least two topics
1	• Explains at least one topic

7. WHS training should be ongoing to keep workers interested and motivated to reduce dangerous behaviour and eliminate hazardous situations.

Marks	Criteria
2	• Good explanation of why WHS training should be ongoing
1	• Mentions at least one point about WHS training

8. Hazard identification and risk assessment is used to evaluate if any particular situation may have the potential to cause harm. They are important so hazards/risks are identified and drastically reduce the likelihood of work-related accidents and ill-health.

Marks	Criteria
3	• Detailed explanation of the importance of hazard identification and risk assessment
2	• Brief explanation of the importance of hazard identification and risk assessment
1	• Mentions one point about hazard identification or risk assessment

9. Hazard identification should be carried out on a regular basis, including:
    - When designing a new process or procedure
    - When installing new machinery
    - Checking equipment/machinery at the beginning or end of each shift
    - Being aware of changes in the performance of equipment/machinery while being operated
    - Regular inspections - timing of these will vary according to the equipment being used
    - After an incident has occurred including near misses and injuries

Marks	Criteria
3	• Explains five or six examples of when hazard identification should take place
2	• Explains three or four examples of when hazard identification should take place
1	• Explains one or two examples of when hazard identification should take place

10. Commonly categories of hazards include:
    - Biological: bacteria, viruses, plants, animals
    - Chemical: including cleaning products, vapours from equipment
    - Ergonomic: setup of workstation, repetitive movements
    - Physical: lighting, temperature, noise, moving objects (like forklifts)
    - Psychological: stress, bullying
    - Safety: trip hazards, equipment breakdowns

Marks	Criteria
6	• Explains 6 categories of hazards
5	• Explains 5 categories of hazards

4	• Explains 4 categories of hazards
3	• Explains 3 categories of hazards
2	• Explains 2 categories of hazards
1	• Explains 1 category of hazard

11. Methods of communication include: bulletin boards, newsletters, letters to individual workers, emails, intranet messages, presentations, briefings, meetings, surveys. One method should be chosen and fully explained.

Marks	Criteria
2	• Good explanation of one method of communicating potential risks to workers
1	• Mentions at least one point about a method of communication

Multiple choice and true/false:

1	2	3	4	5	6	7	8	9	10
a	c	a	c	b	d	c	b	d	a
11	12	13	14	15	16	17	18	19	20
F	T	T	F	T	F	F	T	T	F
21	22	23	24	25	26	27			
T	F	T	T	F	F	T			

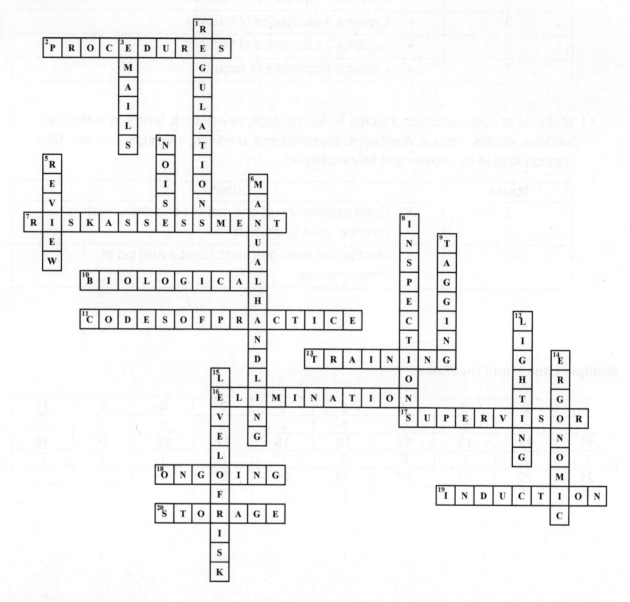

Extended response 1:

a) Answer could include: Policies set out the ideas used as the basis for making decisions, the procedures provide the steps to be followed in specific situations, while the programs state more specifically who will do what and when.

Marks	Criteria
3	• Demonstrates a sound understanding of policies, procedures and programs
2	• Demonstrates a some understanding of policies, procedures and programs
1	• Provides some relevant information

© Five Senses Education Pty Ltd and Linda Joel

b) Answer could include: The primary goal of WHS policies, procedures and programs is to protect workers from foreseen or unforeseen risks. It is important to provide workers with the necessary training with respect to WHS during the induction process, as well as in ongoing training sessions. Training sessions could be in the form of presentations by managers, team briefing or group meetings or one-on-one meetings.

Marks	Criteria
4	• Detailed explanation of WHS policies, procedures and programs and how these are conveyed to workers.
3	• Good explanation of WHS policies, procedures and programs and how these are conveyed to workers.
2	• Identifies some WHS policies, procedures and programs and how these are conveyed to workers.
1	• Provides some relevant information

c) Answer could include: Training should be ongoing to keep workers interested and motivated to reduce dangerous behaviour and eliminate hazardous situations. Frequent hands-on training and practice drives home the message that safety is a critical part of any work site. It is recommended that refresher courses on health and safety matters take place every year to reinforce guidelines and inform workers of new and changing processes. The amount and frequency of training should reflect the level of risk involved. Training specifically needs to be completed when new equipment or substances are purchased, when jobs change, when the work environment changes, when new laws are passed or after an WHS incident has occurred. Training involves explanations, demonstrations, role plays, asking questions, giving feedback, performance assessment, reviewing and following up afterwards.

Marks	Criteria
8	• Demonstrates an extensive knowledge of the importance of ongoing WHS training and how it is best undertaken
6-7	• Demonstrates a thorough knowledge of the importance of ongoing WHS training and how it is best undertaken
4-5	• Demonstrates some knowledge of the importance of ongoing WHS training and how it is best undertaken
2-3	• Demonstrates some knowledge of WHS training AND/OR how it is best undertaken
1	• Provides some relevant information

Extended response 2:

Marks	Criteria
13-15	• Demonstrates an extensive knowledge and understanding of WHS legislation and Industry Codes of Practice as well as workplace policies and procedures within the business services industry • Clearly explains the relationship between WHS legislation and Industry Codes of Conduct with workplace policies and procedures • Communicates ideas and information using relevant workplace examples and industry terminology • Presents a logical and cohesive response
10-12	• Demonstrates a sound knowledge and understanding of WHS legislation and Industry Codes of Practice as well as workplace policies and procedures within the business services industry • Explains the relationship between WHS legislation and Industry Codes of Conduct with workplace policies and procedures • Communicates using relevant workplace examples and industry terminology • Presents a logical response
7-9	• Demonstrates some knowledge and understanding of WHS legislation and Industry Codes of Practice as well as workplace policies and procedures within the business services industry • Shows some relationship between WHS legislation and Industry Codes of Conduct with workplace policies and procedures • Communicates using some workplace examples and industry terminology • Demonstrates some organisation in presenting information
4-6	• Demonstrates basic knowledge and/or understanding of legislation and/or Codes of Practice, and/or workplace policies and procedures • Uses some industry terminology
1-3	• Provides some relevant information

Answer could include:

Legislation and Industry Codes of Practice:
- The Work Health and Safety Act 2011 (NSW)
- The Work Health and Safety Regulation 2017 (NSW)
- The National Code of Practice for the Control of Workplace Hazardous Substances
- The Hazardous Manual Tasks Code of Practice
- How to Manage Work Health and Safety Risks Code of Practice
- The Model Code of Practice for Work Health and Safety Consultation, Co-operation and Co-ordination

All work health and safety issues covered in legislation must be included in organisational policies and procedures and these must be regularly updated accordingly and communicated to all workers. The policy sets out the ideas used as the basis for making decisions while the procedures provide the steps to be followed in specific situations. Policies and procedures could include:
- Risk management
- Responding to incidents, accidents and emergencies
- Reporting processes
- Implementing safe work practices

Chapter 2:

1. A PCBU should consult with workers as worker input and participation improve decision-making about health and safety matters and assists in reducing work-related injuries and disease.

Marks	Criteria
2	• Good explanation of why a PCBU should consult workers about WHS
1	• Mentions at least one point about consulting workers about WHS

2. A safe workplace is more easily achieved when everyone involved in the work communicates with each other to identify hazards and risks, talks about health and safety concerns and works together to find solutions. This includes cooperation between the people who manage or control the work and those who carry out the work or who are affected by the work.

Marks	Criteria
2	• Good explanation of how a safe workplace is achieved
1	• Mentions at least one point about WHS

3. Workers should be consulted when:
   - identifying hazards and assessing the risks to health and safety
   - making decisions about ways to eliminate or minimise those risks
   - making decisions about the adequacy of facilities provided
   - proposing changes, like rearranging the workplace layout or changing shift-work rosters, that may affect health or safety
   - making decisions about procedures for consulting with workers
   - monitoring the health of workers
   - deciding what and when training should occur

Marks	Criteria
3	• Explains five or more examples when workers should be consulted about WHS
2	• Explains three or four examples when workers should be consulted about WHS
1	• Explains one or two examples when workers should be consulted about WHS

4. Informal consultation occurs when taking regular walks around the workplace, talking to workers about any issues they might have and making observations of different work processes. Formal would include having regular meetings with the Health and Safety Representative or the Health and Safety Committee.

Marks	Criteria
2	• Good explanation of both formal and informal consultation
1	• Mentions at least one point about formal or informal consultation

5. Completing a survey is a good method of gathering information about WHS, especially if the survey is anonymous so the workers will be more willing to write what they think without retribution, while providing a quick and easy evaluation of the existing WHS management system and to identify its strengths and weaknesses.

Marks	Criteria
2	• Good explanation of benefits of conducting a survey about WHS
1	• Mentions at least one point about surveys

6. Conducting a safety audit is a means of identifying potential problems before they have an impact on the safety and wellbeing of workers.

Marks	Criteria
2	• Good explanation of benefits of safety audits
1	• Mentions at least one point about safety

7. Hazards can be reported by:
   - Completing a Hazard Report form
   - Reporting hazards to a supervisor or manager
   - Bringing the matter up at a safety meeting or a staff meeting
   - Taking the matter to your Workplace Health and Safety Officer or Representative

Marks	Criteria
2	• Describes three or four ways of reporting hazards
1	• Describes one or two ways of reporting hazards

8. It is important that near misses are reported so that investigation of the potential causes of harm may prevent injuries actually occurring in the future.

Marks	Criteria
2	• Good explanation why near misses should be reported
1	• Mentions at least one point about near misses

9. An incident is an occurrence that interrupts the normal procedure or function in a workplace, generally of minor importance. An accident is an unexpected and undesirable event which usually results in damage or harm to either a worker or business property. An emergency is a serious situation or occurrence that happens unexpectedly and demands immediate action, for example, a fire.

Marks	Criteria
3	• Detailed description of an incident, an accident and an emergency
2	• Basic description of an incident, an accident and an emergency
1	• Mentions at least one point about an incident or an accident or an emergency

11. The more workers are involved in the day-to-day running of a business, the more committed they are to their work and, hence, more productive, and the level of trust in management will increase as they feel that their opinions are being listened to.

Marks	Criteria
2	• Good explanation why workers should be involved in the day-to-day running of a business
1	• Mentions at least one point about workers in a business

12. Open-door communication means that workers can approach managers at any time so they feel that their opinions and concerns will be listened to.

Marks	Criteria
2	• Good explanation of open-door communication
1	• Mentions at least one point about communication

13. Workers should be encouraged to participate in inspections, audits and meetings about safety issues so new issues are identified quickly, moral will increase as workers feel their opinions are taken into account, collaboration increases among team members, more ideas and creative solutions are discussed and teams will more readily accept decisions.

Marks	Criteria
3	• Detailed description of what workers should be encouraged to do and why
2	• Basic description of what workers should be encouraged to do and why
1	• Mentions at least one point about what workers should be encouraged to do

Multiple choice and true/false:

1	2	3	4	5	6	7	8	9	10
c	B	b	c	a	d	a	a	T	F
11	**12**	**13**	**14**	**15**	**16**	**17**	**18**	**19**	**20**
T	T	F	F	T	F	T	T	F	T
21	**22**	**23**	**24**	**25**	**26**	**27**	**28**	**29**	**30**
T	T	F	F	T	F	T	T	T	F

Crossword:

Across

2. ERGONOMICS
7. NEW EQUIPMENT
8. PCBU
9. PROPOSE CHANGES
10. TRUST
11. TALKING TO WORKERS
14. INJURIES
15. NORMAL ROUTINE
19. SURVEY

Down

1. MEETINGS
3. IMMEDIATE ACTION
4. NEARM
5. REGULAR
6. VERBALLY
9. POTENTIAL
12. REFRESHER
12. ENGAGEMENT
13. LIGHTING
16. OPEN DOOR
17. RECTIFIED
18. UNEXPECTED
19. SURVEYORS / CONCERNS

Extended response 1:

1. Answer could include: Workers are directly affected by WHS policies and procedures so consulting with team members will improve decision-making about health and safety issues and assist in reducing work-related injuries and disease. A safe workplace is more easily achieved when team members communicate with each other to identify hazards and risks, talk about health and safety concerns and work together to find solutions. Experienced workers are the ones who are most likely to identify problems as they go about their normal daily routine.

Marks	Criteria
3	• Demonstrates a sound understanding of the importance of consultation in managing WHS
2	• Demonstrates some understanding of the importance of consultation in managing WHS
1	• Provides some relevant information

2. Answer could include: Consultation with team members about WHS can be on a formal or informal basis. Most issues are identified and reported during formal (during meetings or training sessions) and informal discussions (during lunch breaks). Team members can also approach their Health and Safety Representative or a Committee member to raise issues, especially the more serious ones. Team members can also fill out surveys, and if it is anonymous, workers will be more open and frank while not fearing retribution. Team members can also participate in safety audits and inspections and point out where problems can or do occur.

Marks	Criteria
3	• Demonstrates a sound understanding of how team members can contribute to processes when managing WHS
2	• Demonstrates some understanding of how team members can contribute to processes when managing WHS
1	• Provides some relevant information

3. Answer could include: Promptly addressing a health and safety issue with the relevant people affected can increase the chance the matter is resolved efficiently and effectively, while avoiding having to resolve a grievance or dispute if nothing is done. It is everyone's responsibility to look for and identify health and safety issues in the workplace. It is important to immediately report anything that looks hazardous. Answer should also include:
   - Explanation of systems for reporting, including examples
   - Why information needs to be collected, recorded and analysed.

Marks	Criteria
8-9	• Demonstrates an extensive knowledge of why it is important to respond to WHS issues in a timely manner
6-7	• Demonstrates a sound knowledge of why it is important to respond to WHS issues in a timely manner
4-5	• Demonstrates some knowledge of why it is important to respond to WHS issues in a timely manner
2-3	• Demonstrates basic knowledge of WHS issues
1	• Provides some relevant information

Extended response 2:

Answer could include:

- Definition of health and safety issues, including examples
- Definitions of organisational policies and procedures
- Explanation of policies and procedures for:
  - Reporting hazards/risks/issues
  - Monitoring of hazards/risks/issues
  - How WHS issues are handled, depending on whether it is an incident, an accident or an emergency
- When workers should be consulted about policies and procedures, and why they should be consulted.

Marks	Criteria
13-15	• Demonstrates an extensive knowledge of how WHS issues are dealt with according to organisational policies and procedures • Clearly explains the relationship between WHS legislation and Industry Codes of Conduct with workplace policies and procedures • Communicates ideas and information using relevant workplace examples and industry terminology
10-12	• Demonstrates a sound knowledge of how WHS issues are dealt with according to organisational policies and procedures • Explains the relationship between WHS legislation and Industry Codes of Conduct with workplace policies and procedures • Communicates using relevant workplace examples and industry terminology

7-9	• Demonstrates some knowledge of how WHS issues are dealt with according to organisational policies and procedures • Shows some relationship between WHS legislation and Industry Codes of Conduct with workplace policies and procedures • Communicates using some relevant workplace examples and industry terminology
4-6	• Demonstrates basic knowledge of WHS issues AND/OR organisational policies and procedures • Uses some industry terminology
1-3	• Provides some relevant information

Chapter 3:

1. Work roles for which specific training must be completed include:
   • First aid
   • Health and Safety Representative
   • White Card for construction industry
   • High Risk Work training and assessment for jobs where there is a high risk of death, injury or illness if/when exposed to a hazard
   • Asbestos Assessment or Removal training
   • WHS entry Permit Holder training for Union Officials

Marks	Criteria
3	• Identifies five to six work roles that require specific training
2	• Identifies two to four work roles that require specific training
1	• Identifies at least one work role that require specific training

2. The level of risk determines the amount and frequency of training.

Marks	Criteria
1	• Identifies that level of risk determines training

3. Health and Safety training should include:
   - Who are the health and safety representative and the first aid officer; location of the first aid station
   - Hazard and risk identification and reporting
   - What happens if hurt on the job and Worker's Compensation requirements
   - Awareness of the consequences of poor safety with regards to legislative action, team morale and impact on the business

Marks	Criteria
3	- Detailed explanation of a range of topics covered in WHS training
2	- Explains at least two topics covered in WHS training
1	- Mentions at least one point about training

4. Training Needs Analysis finds the gap between competencies that exist (what is) and what competencies are required (the ideal), and if that gap can be removed or reduced by training.

Marks	Criteria
2	- Good explanation of a Training Needs Analysis
1	- Mentions at least one point about training

5. Refresher training is important to ensure all are reminded of requirements of such things as emergency and/or evacuation procedures, first aid, and manual handling techniques.

Marks	Criteria
2	- Good explanation of why refresher training is important
1	- Mentions at least one point about training

6. Levels of training are:
   - Level 1: Provision of information, which is typically induction level information, but can also include information relating to compliance with legislation, policy or procedures.
   - Level 2: Proficiency training, including being trained against a Safe Work Procedure while working under supervision, as a control measure, until deemed proficient by the supervisor.
   - Level 3: Competency based training to assess knowledge against skill-based competencies which results in the attainment of a certificate or licence, for example, before being able to operate a forklift.

Marks	Criteria
3	• Good explanation of the three levels of training
2	• Brief explanation of at least two levels of training
1	• Explains one level of training

7. COVID-19 has changed training from being delivered face-to-face to via "connected real-time delivery", using live video streaming/conferencing platforms like Zoom and Skype.

Marks	Criteria
2	• Good explanation of how training has changed
1	• Mentions at least one point about training

8. Supervision must be provided, where appropriate, for work team members who are not deemed competent to undertake a task or work process to ensure the safety of the worker, to meet WHS obligations and prevent incidents.

Marks	Criteria
2	• Good explanation of why some workers are supervised on the job
1	• Mentions at least one point about supervision

Multiple choice and true/false:

1	2	3	4	5	6	7	8	9	10
a	b	b	a	c	d	b	b	F	T
11	**12**	**13**	**14**	**15**	**16**	**17**	**18**	**19**	**20**
T	F	T	F	F	F	T	T	T	F

Crossword:

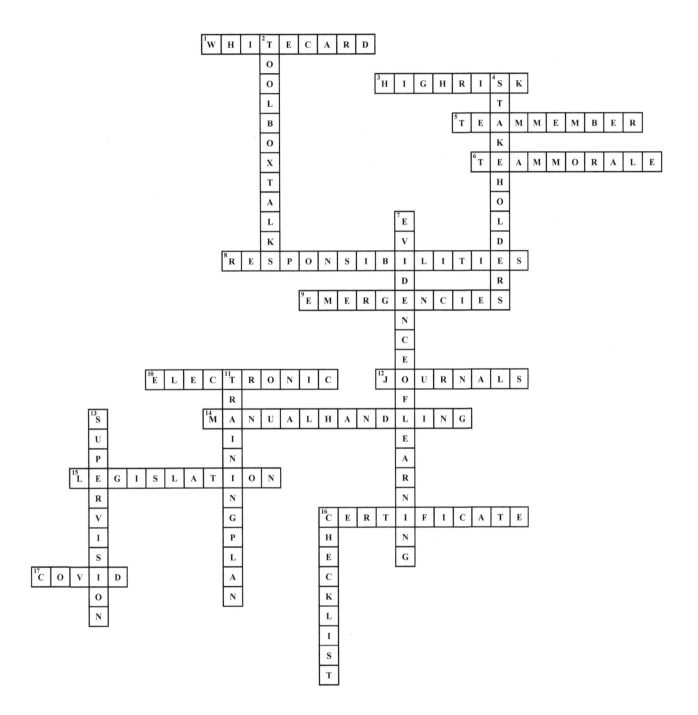

Across:
1. WHITECARD
3. HIGHRISK
5. TEAMMEMBER
6. TEAMMORALE
8. RESPONSIBILITIES
9. EMERGENCIES
10. ELECTRONIC
12. JOURNALS
14. MANUALHANDLING
15. LEGISLATION
16. CERTIFICATE
17. COVID

Down:
2. TOOLBOXTALK
4. STAKEHOLD
7. EVIDENCE
11. TRAININGPLAN
13. SUPERVISION

Extended response 1:

a) Answer could include:
- WHS legislation, regulations and codes of practice stipulate workers must complete specified training and assessment before they can undertake certain work or roles, and include examples
- Training closes the gap between what skills are required and what skills the team members have

Marks	Criteria
3	• Demonstrates a sound understanding of the importance of WHS training
2	• Demonstrates some understanding of the importance of WHS training
1	• Provides some relevant information

b) Answer could include: Supervision must be provided for work team members who are not deemed competent to undertake a task or work process, to provide adequate direction and oversight to ensure the safety of the worker, to meet WHS obligations and prevent incidents. If inadequacies are detected, on-the-spot awareness training is a good idea. Specific training can also be provided as well as "toolbox talks" that focus on a specific hazard or risk.

Marks	Criteria
3	• Demonstrates a sound understanding of how team members can be supported with training
2	• Demonstrates some understanding of how team members can be supported with training
1	• Provides some relevant information

c) Answer could include:
- Level 1 training: Provision of information, which is typically induction level information, but can also include information relating to compliance with legislation, policy or procedures. Provision of information can be verbal, written, electronic or given in a presentation. Most WHS training in the Business Services work environment comes under this level.
- Level 2 training: Proficiency training, including being trained against a Safe Work Procedure while working under supervision, as a control measure, until deemed proficient by the supervisor.
- Level 3 training: Competency based training to assess knowledge against skill-based competencies which results in the attainment of a certificate or licence, for example, before being able to operate a forklift.

Although WHS laws do not specify how training must be delivered, in practice, most WHS regulators require training be delivered face-to-face. COVID has impacted methods of training since 2020, so delivery methods have changed. It has become the "norm" for most WHS training to be completed via "connected real-time delivery", using live video streaming / conferencing platforms like Zoom and Skype. Benefits of connected real-time delivery include:

- Involves real time interaction between trainer and learner
- Provides for active participation between trainer and learner
- Verification of evidence for learning can still be done via video conferencing
- Direct observations and verbal assessment are still possible

Unfortunately, this method of delivery does not allow self-paced learning as everyone must keep up with the trainer and it cannot include pre-recorded training videos. Training for certain jobs is not suitable via connected real-time delivery, such as high-risk jobs and asbestos removal, which must complete their training face-to-face.

Marks	Criteria
8-9	• Demonstrates an extensive knowledge of levels of training and how these have changed
6-7	• Demonstrates a sound knowledge of levels of training and how these have changed
4-5	• Demonstrates some knowledge of levels of training and how these have changed
2-3	• Demonstrates basic knowledge of training
1	• Provides some relevant information

Chapter 4:

Short answers:

1. A hazard is anything that can cause harm to a person.

Marks	Criteria
1	• Provides an accurate definition of a hazard

2. Hazard identification is the process of examining the workplace to identify all potentially hazardous things or situations that may cause harm to workers, customers, clients or visitors to the workplace.

Marks	Criteria
2	• Good explanation of hazard identification
1	• Mentions at least one point about hazards

3. Hazards are likely to be found in the physical work environment; in using equipment, materials or substances; in the way work tasks are performed; and in the management of work design.

Marks	Criteria
2	• Good explanation of where hazards could be found
1	• Mentions at least one point about hazards

4. Human factors: boxes stacked precariously (they could fall on someone); filing cabinets being left open (causing injury); spills not being mopped up (can cause slips and falls resulting in sprains and fractures)

Marks	Criteria
3	• Good explanation of three human factors that can be a hazard in an office
2	• Good explanation of two human factors that can be a hazard in an office
1	• Explains one human factor that can be a hazard in an office

5. Not only should hazards be reported, but also incidents and near misses.

Marks	Criteria
2	• Mentions at least two things other than hazards that should be reported
1	• Mentions one other thing that should be reported

6. A risk assessment works out how likely a risk or hazard could harm someone and how serious the harm could be.

Marks	Criteria
2	• Good explanation of risk assessment
1	• Mentions at least one point about risks

7. Risk control involves managing hazards before people are hurt or become ill, or there is damage to the plant, property or to the environment.

Marks	Criteria
2	• Good explanation of risk control
1	• Mentions at least one point about risks

8. The most effective method for controlling risks is to eliminate the risk altogether by not purchasing hazardous materials, plant or equipment and to redesign the workplace and work systems to eliminate risks.

Marks	Criteria
2	• Good explanation of controlling risks
1	• Mentions at least one point about risks

9. Risks can be minimised by:

    a. Substitution: using something with a lower risk (Eg. making the load lighter by using smaller boxes)

    b. Modification: changing work practices (Eg. introducing job rotation to vary repetitive work)

    c. Isolation: isolating the source of the risk (Eg. enclosing noisy machines like photocopiers within a soundproof booth)

    d. Engineering control: introducing safeguards (Eg. using a mechanical device to handle a heavy or awkward object)

Marks	Criteria
3	• Good explanation of three or more ways to minimise risks
2	• Good explanation of two ways to minimise risks
1	• Explains one way to minimise risks

10. Safe work practices include introducing job rotation to restrict hours worked on difficult jobs and conducting more staff training in the correct operating procedures; taking adequate rest breaks, especially when constantly using computers.

Marks	Criteria
2	• Good explanation of two safe work practices
1	• Explains one safe work practice

11. Hazard assessment and control measures should be reviewed when there is a change to the workplace including when new work systems, tools, machinery or equipment are introduced.

Marks	Criteria
2	• Good explanation of when hazard assessment and control measures should be reviewed
1	• Mentions at least one point about hazard assessment or control measures

12. Further inadequacies can be identified through internal and external audits, feedback from team members or other staff, when implementing innovative changes, when WHS legislation is changed and through the consultative process with workers.

Marks	Criteria
3	• Good explanation of how further inadequacies can be identified
2	• Some explanation of how further inadequacies can be identified
1	• Mentions at least one point about identifying inadequacies

13. Any inadequacies found should be reported to fellow team members, the supervisor, the manager or PCBU, or to the WHS representative or committee.

Marks	Criteria
2	• Identifies more than one person to whom reports of inadequacies should be made
1	• Identifies one person to whom reports of inadequacies should be made

14. Accident and incident reports can identify when an injury or disease becomes common, as a sharp increase in the number of injuries in an area can mean there is a problem that needs to be addressed.

Marks	Criteria
2	• Identifies what can be identified by accident and incident reports
1	• Mentions one point about accident or report forms

15. Incidents can include property damage, theft or security-related issues, accidents, injuries as well as "near misses".

Marks	Criteria
2	• Good explanation of an incident
1	• Mentions one point about incidents

16. Notifiable incidents include a death, a serious injury or illness, or a dangerous incident that exposes any person to a serious risk, even if no one is injured.

Marks	Criteria
2	• Good explanation of when an incident must be reported
1	• Mentions one point about incidents and/or SafeWork NSW

Multiple choice and true/false:

1	2	3	4	5	6	7	8	9	10
b	a	b	b	c	d	c	a	c	c
11	**12**	**13**	**14**	**15**	**16**	**17**	**18**	**19**	**20**
d	b	b	T	F	F	F	T	F	T
21	**22**	**23**	**24**	**25**	**26**	**27**	**28**	**29**	**30**
T	F	F	F	T	T	T	T	F	F

Crossword:

Extended response 1:

a) Answer could include: Examples of potential workplace hazards in a business services environment include:
- Noisy machinery that could damage hearing
- Frayed electrical cords or using too many power cords on the one power point which may result in shorts or electrical shocks
- Fumes from equipment like photocopiers can result in workers feeling ill or experiencing headaches
- Boxes stacked precariously could fall on someone; filing cabinets being left open can cause injury; spills not being mopped up which can cause slips and falls resulting in sprains and fractures
- Items being lifted incorrectly, causing back strain
- Ripped/worn carpets causing falls; glare and/or inappropriate lighting can cause eye problems and headaches
- Unrealistic timeframes resulting in stress, headaches, low productivity; physical layout of office not practical which can cause time wastage and higher stress levels

Marks	Criteria
3	• Demonstrates a sound understanding of potential workplace hazards
2	• Demonstrates some understanding of workplace hazards
1	• Provides some relevant information

b) Answer could include: A risk assessment should include:
- Identification of the factors that may be contributing to the risk
- Reviewing any health and safety information that is available from an authoritative source which is relevant to the particular hazard (particularly for chemicals)
- Evaluation of how severe the harm could be: includes looking at the types of injuries/illnesses/harm/damage that could result from the hazard; how often the task is completed and in what conditions; the number of people who could be exposed to the hazard and for how long; and the possible effects from exposure to the hazard
- Evaluation of how a hazard may cause harm: includes examining how work is completed, whether existing control measures are in place and whether they control the harm
- Identify the actions necessary to eliminate or control the risk
- Keeping necessary records to ensure that the risks are eliminated or controlled

Marks	Criteria
3	• Demonstrates a sound understanding of the process of risk assessment
2	• Demonstrates some understanding of risk assessment
1	• Provides some relevant information

c) Answer could include: Risk control involves managing hazards before people are hurt or become ill, or there is damage to the plant, property or to the environment. When controlling a risk, the most effective approach is using a hierarchy of control as it acts on the risks in the environment rather than on the people.

The hierarchy for risk control is:
- Eliminate the risk: the most effective method for controlling risks is to eliminate the risk altogether. The best way to eliminate risks is to not purchase hazardous materials, plant or equipment and to redesign the workplace and work systems to eliminate risks.
- Minimise the risk: if risks cannot be eliminated, they must be reduced as much as possible. The best ways to do this include:
  - Substitution: using something with a lower risk (Eg. making the load lighter by using smaller boxes)
  - Modification: changing work practices (Eg. introducing job rotation to vary repetitive work)
  - Isolation: isolating the source of the risk (Eg. enclosing noisy machines like photocopiers within a soundproof booth)
- Engineering control: introducing safeguards (Eg. using a mechanical device to handle a heavy or awkward object)

Other controls include:

- Administration: could develop work methods or procedures to reduce the conditions of risk; ensure all new workers complete appropriate induction training; carrying out regular drills so workers know how to deal with emergency situations; conducting risk assessments on a regular basis
- Safe work practices: introduce job rotation to restrict hours worked on difficult jobs and conduct more staff training in the correct operating procedures; taking adequate rest breaks, especially when constantly using computers
- Personal protective equipment (PPE): the use of equipment such as safety glasses, gloves, helmets and ear muffs can protect workers from hazards when handling such things as handling chemicals or working in a noisy environment

Marks	Criteria
8-9	• Demonstrates an extensive knowledge of risk control
6-7	• Demonstrates a sound knowledge of risk control
4-5	• Demonstrates some knowledge of risk control
2-3	• Demonstrates basic knowledge of risk control
1	• Provides some relevant information

Extended response 2:

Answer could include:

Hazard identification, risk assessment and control is an ongoing process as it is important to regularly review the effectiveness of hazard assessment and control measures, especially when there is a change to the workplace including when new work systems, tools, machinery or equipment are introduced. Additional training and supervision should be provided for all new workers.

Evaluation should take place to ensure that existing control measures are:
- Effective
- Safe to follow
- Introduced safely
- Reviewed to ensure that all potential and existing hazards are identified
- Not superseded with new work methods, equipment or chemicals to make the process safer
- Clearly communicated to all workers
- Understood so workers can identify and minimise risks
- Meeting legislative requirements

It is important to keep records according to WHS legislative requirements. An WHS incident report is an official document that records the key details of an incident in the workplace, like property damage, theft or security-related issues, accidents, injuries as well as "near misses". An incident report should be completed at the time an incident occurs, no matter how minor it is, even if no injuries occur. Information recorded on the form include:
- Details of person/people injured
- Details of sustained injuries
- Name of the person who reported the incident
- Description of incident: location, date, time, incident details/type of incident
- Causes of the incident
- Whether police or WHS authorities were notified
- Follow up recommendations

Accident/incident reports will identify when an injury or disease becomes common. If there is a sharp increase in the number of injuries in an area, there is obviously a problem with the area that needs to be addressed. Incidents can compromise the safety of workers and can happen in any business, regardless of its size, location or industry. Reporting all incidents is important for the simple reason that if they are not reported, the PCBU will not know there is a problem that needs addressing. Records should be kept for a minimum of five years.

Marks	Criteria
13-15	• Demonstrates an extensive knowledge of hazard identification, risk assessment and control and keeping records according to WHS legislative requirements
10-12	• Demonstrates a sound knowledge of hazard identification, risk assessment and control and keeping records according to WHS legislative requirements
7-9	• Demonstrates a sound knowledge of hazard identification, risk assessment and control and keeping records according to WHS legislative requirements
4-6	• Demonstrates basic knowledge of WHS issues AND/OR keeping records
1-3	• Provides some relevant information

Chapter 5:

Note: These tasks are not awarded marks. Submitted answers will be marked as competent or not yet competent. Any task that is deemed not yet competent must be reviewed, updated and resubmitted until it has been deemed competent. Record the date when deemed competent.

Task	Competent	Not yet competent
Task 1: policy 1		
Task 1: policy 2		
Task 1: policy 3		
Task 1: addendum		
Task 2: teams		
Task 2: hazards		
Task 2: WHS policies and procedures		
Task 2: legislation, regulations and codes of practice		
Task 2: organisational systems and procedures		

Notes

_____

_____

_____

_____

_____

_____

_____

_____

_____

_____

_____

_____

_____

_____

_____

_____

_____

_____

_____

_____

_____

_____

_____

_____

_____

_____

_____

_____